A SERIES FOR NEW YORK

WOODFORD PRESS, *San Francisco*
Produced in partnership with
MAJOR LEAGUE BASEBALL PROPERTIES, INC.

AN OFFICIAL PUBLICATION OF MAJOR LEAGUE BASEBALL

A SERIES FOR
NEW YORK

Contents

New Era Cap Company's 59/50 Authentic Diamond Collection caps are the only caps worn by all Major League Baseball players on the field of play. These caps are 100% made in the USA to exacting standards set by Major League Baseball. The Authentic Diamond Collection caps, the *genuine* article, are available to fans at sporting goods stores, department stores and ballparks across the country and around the world.

New Era is also the exclusive manufacturer of the first ever official 1996 World Series on-field cap, worn by the New York Yankees and the Atlanta Braves during all games of the 1996 World Series, as well as the official World Series Championship Clubhouse caps worn by the New York Yankees at the conclusion of the

World Series. These three caps commemorate the great accomplishments achieved in 1996 by both the Atlanta Braves and the New York Yankees. New Era congratulates both teams on their achievements and for providing all baseball fans a series to remember for years to come.

WOODFORD PRESS
660 Market Street, San Francisco, CA 94104

Book design by Laurence J. Hyman

Produced in partnership with and licensed by
MAJOR LEAGUE BASEBALL PROPERTIES, INC.

ISBN: 0-942627-27-X ISSN: 1088-7202
First Printing: November 1996
Printed and bound in the United States of America

THE YANKEES' ROAD TO THE SERIES

By Joe Gergen
Newsday

It doesn't make everything right with the world that the Yankees have returned to the top for the first time in 18 years. But it certainly has made New York a cheerier place, its raw energy transformed into small-town enthusiasm for a team that reflected the city's self-image of succeeding under intense pressure. Diminished crime rates don't provide a rallying point for civic pride.

The Yankees' coronation shouldn't be regarded as a surprise. After all, the team had the highest payroll in organized baseball and led its division from April 30

clear through September. What made the journey so extraordinary was Joe Torre's ability to forge so many personalities into a cohesive unit almost overnight. The process began in Spring Training and contributors were acquired in July and August, and David Cone didn't rejoin the starting rotation until September following surgery for an aneurysm in his pitching shoulder.

In all probability, no playoff team in history has undergone such a complete overhaul as that performed on the 1995 Yankees. Despite the franchise's first Post Season appearance in 14 years, George Steinbrenner

Newsday SPORTS

WEDNESDAY, MAY 1, 1996

Birds Bashed

Yankees starter Andy Pettitte was browbeaten after allowing nine runs in one-plus inning.

Pitchers are endangered species as Yankees rip O's staff for 17 hits, three HRs in 13-10 win

DAVID LENNON'S STORY ON PAGE A82

In a bit of foreshadowing, the Yankees belted the Orioles on April 30 in their first game of the year at Camden Yards. New York would not lose a game at Baltimore's home park the entire season, including the playoffs.

An improbable comeback was complete. Dwight Gooden, the former Mets' hurler who hadn't pitched in the Major Leagues for nearly two seasons, no-hit the powerful Seattle Mariners at Yankee Stadium on May 14, winning the game, 2-0.

ewsday

THE LONG ISLAND NEWSPAPER

50¢

WEDNESDAY, MAY 15, 1996 • NASSAU

Dr. No!

Gooden No-Hits Mariners, 2-0

Sports

transferred GM Gene Michael and made an offer that Manager Buck Showalter could and did refuse. Their successors, Bob Watson and Torre, set about reshaping the club to their specifications with free-agent additions and trades, not all well-received. They also provided encouragement to youngsters that Michael had nurtured in the burgeoning farm system.

Derek Jeter, a rookie shortstop, was one of five new position players that started the season. The early

continued on page 10

8

Gooden celebrates with teammates at Yankee Stadium.

Newsday SPORTS

MONDAY, JULY 29, 1996

Darryl Strawberry watches flight of his two-run blast, off Jason Jacome, his first home run since July 13.

300 HitteR

STORY ON PAGE A48

Another former Mets player who looked good in pinstripes was slugger Darryl Strawberry. On July 28 at Yankee Stadium, he hit a game-winning, two-run homer in the bottom of the ninth inning. It was the 300th home run of his career.

In May, David Cone underwent aneurysm surgery in his pitching arm. On September 2 in Oakland, he miraculously returned to action by throwing seven no-hit innings before manager Joe Torre removed him from the game.

U.S. Dominates · Romps Russia / Page A48

Newsday SPORTS

TUESDAY, SEPT. 3, 1996

On May 10, David Cone underwent surgery to repair an aneurysm in his shoulder. Yesterday, the A's couldn't touch him in Yanks' one-hit, 5-0 win.

Cone throws unhittable stuff in storybook return to mound

Magnificent Seven

COVERAGE BY LENNON, GERGEN AND HEYMAN BEGINS ON PAGE A58

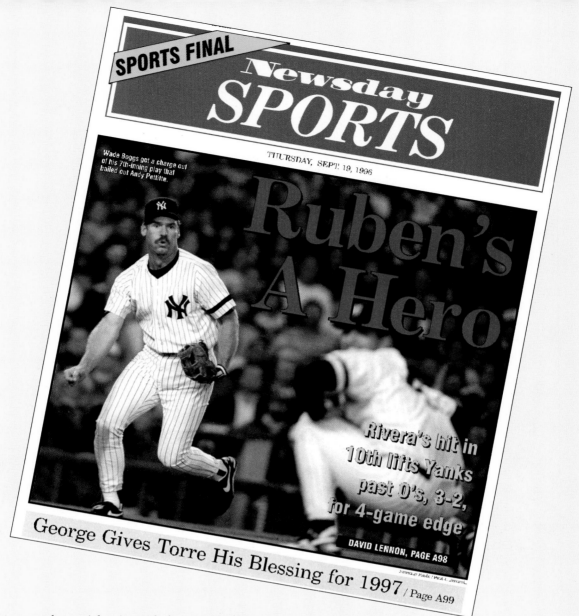

Newsday SPORTS

THURSDAY, SEPT. 19, 1996

Wade Boggs got a charge out of his 7th-inning play that bailed out Andy Pettitte.

Ruben's A Hero

Rivera's hit in 10th lifts Yanks past O's, 3-2, for 4-game edge

DAVID LENNON, PAGE A98

George Gives Torre His Blessing for 1997 / Page A99

In the first game of a crucial series with the second-place Orioles at Yankee Stadium on September 18, rookie Ruben Rivera's soft single to rightfield in the 10th inning lifted the Yankees to a stirring 3-2 victory.

reliance on so-called "little ball"—the bunt, hit-and-run, double steal—was mitigated by the arrival of Darryl Strawberry and then Cecil Fielder. But the characteristic resilience and tenacity was not altered. The Yankees outlasted the Baltimore Orioles, 13-10, in the longest nine-inning game in Major League history (four hours, 21 minutes) on April 30 to take control of the American League East. Six months later, they overcame a 6-0 deficit and handed the Atlanta Braves a devastating 8-6, 10-inning defeat in the longest World Series game ever played (4:17).

They would not be denied when they traveled. Against the two opponents regarded as the strongest in

their league, the Orioles and Cleveland Indians, and the 1995 champion Braves, they won all 18 road games in 1996. They also won each of the eight Post Season games played away from Yankee Stadium, an unprecedented achievement.

Along the way, they also favored New York with some memorable moments: Doc Gooden's no-hitter in May; the four-game sweep of the Orioles at Camden Yards in July; Strawberry's 300th career homer that defeated Kansas City in the final turn at bat; Cone's apparently miraculous seven hitless innings against Oakland on Labor Day; Ruben Rivera's stunning layout catch that reversed the team's slide in Detroit and his pinch hit

Newsday
SPORTS
Sunday, October 6, 1996

SUNDAY SPECIAL
Chris Childs: Knicks'
Comeback Kid

Knockout Punch

Bernie homers twice as Yanks down Rangers, advance to ALCS

COVERAGE BEGINS PAGES B2-3

Bernie Williams' second home run closed out the scoring in the Yankees' 6-4 clinching victory over the Rangers.

Alomar, O's Eliminate Indians
ALCS GAME 1
Orioles at Yankees
Tuesday, 8:07 p.m.

NL SWEEPS: GLAVINE, BRAVES COAST PAST LA; JORDAN'S HR ELIMINATES PADRES

On October 5 in Arlington, Texas, switch-hitting center fielder Bernie Williams hit a home run from each side of the plate in a 6-4 victory over the Rangers that clinched the Division Series for the Yankees.

eight nights later that slowed the charge of the Orioles; and the 19-2 romp over Milwaukee that clinched the first division title since 1980.

They were no longer the Bronx Bombers, at least not in the era of "arena baseball." They had no individual to stand toe-to-toe with Juan Gonzalez in the Division Series, but he was a Lone Ranger against an army. The Orioles boasted the greatest bashers in Major League history, at least statistically, but the pitching of Jimmy Key and Andy Pettitte reduced their big bats to matchsticks. The Braves had three starting pitchers to die for, so the Yankees turned each Atlanta miscue into a run, raked its suspect bullpen and exploited its weak bench.

Bernie Williams, the home-grown center fielder, was brilliant in the first two rounds of the playoffs, and Fielder wielded a club in the World Series. The Yankees' bullpen was brilliant throughout. The team got an enormous lift from Jim Leyritz, a superb performance from Pettitte, and a big hit from Joe Girardi. And even the much-maligned Graeme Lloyd lent a helping hand to Mariano Rivera and MVP John Wetteland in three victories, including the 3-2 finale. In lieu of Mr. October, there are 25 Messrs. October.

Meanwhile, the manager with the perpetual five o'clock shadow and the deep-set eyes put the best possible face on a franchise that had been viewed as

THURSDAY, OCT. 10, 1996

ALCS GAME 1

Jeff Maier, 12, leans over wall above RF Tony Tarasco and helps turn Derek Jeter's fly ball into HR.

Grabby young fan helps Yanks come back before Bernie's HR wins it in 11th

COVERAGE BEGINS ON A98

Kid Glove Treatment

anything but warm during Steinbrenner's reign. Torre was a Brooklyn native whose quest for fulfillment after more than three decades in the sport and whose evenhanded treatment of all in the face of family crises captivated the city. People from all over the metropolitan area who had vowed never again to care dusted off their old navy blue caps with the interlocking "NY" and wore them around town.

The Yankees are champions again. Start spreading the news.

The most controversial play of the Post Season came on October 9 at Yankee Stadium when a 12-year- old boy reached over the fence and pulled Derek Jeter's fly ball into the seats for a game-tying home run in the eighth inning.

On October 13, the Yankees beat the Orioles, 6-4, to win the ALCS in five games and earn their first World Series trip since 1981. Fittingly, their celebration came on the road, where they were unbeaten in postseason play.

Newsday
THE LONG ISLAND NEWSPAPER

http://www.newsday.com   MONDAY, OCT. 14, 1996 • SUFFOLK   50¢

FLAG DAY !

From left, Wade Boggs, John Wetteland, Tino Martinez and Jim Leyritz celebrate 6-4 victory

See You At The Series

YANKS WIN PENNANT WITH POWER SURGE IN BALTIMORE

A SERIES FOR NEW YORK

Among the Best Ever Played

By Bruce Jenkins

The 1996 World Series began in a rainstorm and finished like a scene from "Oklahoma." It opened to flooded New York streets and ended with a ticker-tape parade. It could have been called after Game 2, due to lack of interest, and it wound up a Classic.

Only the New York Yankees could have made this possible. For nearly a half-century, they won World Championships with an almost inevitable dominance. But they won this one from the backstretch, and much of the city wept. Somehow, out of the cosmopolitan swirl of The Big Apple, a haughty tradition and a $60 million payroll, a small-town story was born.

All around the country, people were touched by the Yankees like never before. People from hated Boston to jaded Hollywood. People from Brooklyn, for crying out loud. Old Dodgers fans shook their heartbreak and the memories of Ebbets Field to embrace the 1996 Yankees, a team for all tastes. The Yanks win the Series. It's a story that goes back to Ruthian times, as familiar as the sunrise. But it was never like this.'

The old Yankees were a three-run homer by Gehrig or Mantle, a two-hitter by Ford, a great catch by DiMaggio, a 10-1 lead in the third. Now batting, Yogi Berra. How many years did he play in this thing, twenty? Some of the great Yankees had better careers in the World Series than other players crafted in a lifetime. They were bold, heroic and classy. But few joyful tears were shed on their behalf.

By the time the Yankees beat the Atlanta Braves, 3-2, in the riveting sixth game at Yankee Stadium, every baseball fan in the country knew the heart-wrenching story of Joe Torre and his brothers. They knew all the underdogs, all the ones who played hurt, everyone who had come back from severe personal setbacks. These were the Yankees? It felt more like an old Jimmy Stewart movie. Suddenly the Yanks stood for warmth, hard work, unselfishness, faith, loyalty—and they weren't afraid to cry. For a single, unforgettable autumn, they were the most likeable team in sports.

They were the first team to win four straight World Series games after losing the first two at home, thus forging the most dramatic turnaround in Series history. They went 8-0 on the Post Season road through Texas, Baltimore and Atlanta. They won the 23rd world championship in franchise history. But historical footnotes couldn't match the lovely Tuesday morning of October 29, when New York City looked like something out of an old, forgotten newsreel. More than three million people were on hand, lining the streets, leaning out of windows, hanging from poles, to watch the champions' victory parade go by. With the memories so fresh and vivid, it was a time to cherish the games and the many priceless stories in the Yankees dugout.

There went Darryl Strawberry, who pulled himself from the depths of substance abuse, toiled in the mid-summer obscurity of the Northern League and played the

World Series with a broken toe. Dwight Gooden, Strawberry's partner in sobriety, the man who pitched a no-hitter in May and had a memorable 11-2 run before his arm gave out. David Cone, who underwent risky and painstaking surgery for the removal of an aneurysm and was back on the mound just four months later.

There went Jimmy Key, who got the win in Game 6 after proposing to his fiancée that very afternoon. Cecil Fielder and Charlie Hayes, stuck with last-place teams as late as July. Joe Girardi and Jim Leyritz, the blue-collar catchers who made Yankees fans forget popular Mike Stanley. Series MVP John Wetteland, a self-described "hellion" who found a clean-and-sober, deeply religious lifestyle and became the American League's best short reliever.

They went by non-stop, each man a separate novel. Graeme Lloyd, who watched his first World Series at the age of 12 on his father's sheep ranch in Australia, had been the most unpopular Yankees player in September. He arrived from Milwaukee with a sore elbow and described his regular season outings as "the worst three weeks of my life." He was now a hero, a lanky left-hander with a Down Under accent and his own cult following.

Wade Boggs had reached the type of closure found only in those children's sports books with corny titles such as "A Home Run for Billy." Boggs was the man crying in the Shea Stadium dugout after the 1986 World Series, lamenting the Red Sox' unspeakable demise and the loss of his mother to a car accident just weeks before. Now he was back in New York, across town and a winner, almost exactly ten years later. "I swear, when we rushed onto the field after the final out, I looked up into the sky and saw my mother smiling down on me," said Boggs, his eyes not quite dry, in the victorious clubhouse.

Paul O'Neill welcomed his automobile ride through town, a luxury he never had in the outfield. O'Neill played the whole of October on a strained hamstring, an injury so painful that he had to be helped off the airplane bringing the Yankees back to New York for Game 6. There was Tino Martinez, who stepped into Don Mattingly's formidable shadow and drove in 117 runs during the season; Mariano Rivera, who came back from elbow surgery to become the most fabled "setup man" in relief-pitching history; and Bob Watson, the first African-American general manager to preside over a World Series Championship team and a man who feared for his job during the team's late-season slump.

"This whole team is such a New York story," Cone said after the Series. "It's a comeback team, top to bottom. The list of stories is incredible. You'd love to be a writer with a team like this. Just pick a story line and run with it."

The litany of human interest doesn't even mention the team's young stars: Rookie of the Year shortstop Derek Jeter, 21-game winner Andy Pettite or stylish Bernie Williams, who plays classical guitar and center field with equal panache. Nor is it complete without acknowledging the most compelling Yankees story of them all, the sad eyes of manager Joe Torre.

The Torres came from a red-brick house on Avenue T in Brooklyn. Joe and his brothers, Rocco and Frank, were all ballplayers. They came from a time when kids had to fight their way onto the crowded sandlots, when baseball truly was the national pastime. They played against the sons of working-class families, the Italian, Irish and Jewish laborers of the neighborhood, and they starred on the Cadets, a storied amateur team out of Brooklyn's Marine Park.

Rocco was the oldest. They say he had potential as a pitcher before he was swept off by the Navy for World War II, and he later joined the New York police force. Frank was a talented first baseman who signed with the Milwaukee Braves and played in the 1957 and 1958 World Series against the Yankees. Although he was mostly a backup to Joe Adcock, Frank hit home runs off Tom Sturdivant and Bob Turley during the Braves' seven-game run to the 1957 championship.

Joe was always on the periphery of the World Series. He joined the Braves in 1960, too late for the glory years. He was traded to the St. Louis Cardinals in 1969, just in time to miss their back-to-back World Series appearances. He played on some nondescript Mets teams, and in 15 seasons as a manager, he got close to the Series just once, guiding the 1982 Braves into the National League playoffs. He kept missing October. In a generous attempt to soothe his little brother's envy, Frank gave Joe one of his World Series rings. But it wasn't the same. It wasn't like being there.

"I guess what happened," Torre joked later, "is that God was waiting for me to put on the pinstripes."

For the Yankees' fans and players, the summer of 1996 took on a mythical, dream-like quality. For Joe Torre, it became a nightmare. In June, brother Rocco was watching the Yanks play on television when he collapsed in his living room and died of a heart attack. It was sudden, completely unexpected; Joe found out in the middle of a doubleheader at Cleveland. He hurried back to New York for the funeral, where he placed a baseball and a Yankees lineup card into the casket. It was sufficiently difficult to deal with Rocco's passing, but then Frank's heart grew weak, as well. He took a room at Columbia Presbyterian Hospital to wait for a heart transplant, and the days turned into weeks. His gaunt, increasingly withered countenance haunted Joe on every visit.

"This whole summer has taken a lot of the enjoyment out of it," Torre said in late September. "My brothers were more like fathers to me, the way they always looked after me. Continuing to manage has been like jumping in a foxhole, pulling the cover over your head, keeping out reality. My wife still thinks I haven't grieved for the loss of Rocco, and she might be right. Baseball has been my place to hide."

Then came a sparkling afternoon at Camden Yards, Game 5 of the American League Championship Series. That's the day Joe came out of hiding and went straight to the World Series. As the Yankees polished off their 8-4 victory over the Baltimore Orioles, it was remarkable to consider how many of Torre's colleagues had been to the World Series: a half-dozen players, the owner, the general manager (Watson was a Yankees player in the team's previous World Series appearance, 1981), and all six coaches: Mel Stottlemyre, Don Zimmer, Willie Randolph, Chris Chambliss, Jose Cardenal and Tony Cloninger.

The moment was not lost on any of these men. While the victorious Yankees celebrated wildly on the field, Torre was mobbed in the dugout by all of those coaches and Reggie Jackson, Mr. October himself, an assistant to Steinbrenner. Torre couldn't stop crying, and they all cried with him, and it was difficult to remember a more poignant baseball scene. From that day on, Torre's Yankees belonged to everyone.

While the Yankees stormed into the World Series with a three-game sweep in

" I thought it (Yankee Stadium) would be in black and white ."
—Greg Maddux

"That Babe was some architect."
—Chipper Jones

Baltimore, the Braves were taking on the look of a dynasty. Already veterans of three World Series in the 1990s, they came back from a 3-1 deficit to crush the St. Louis Cardinals over the final three games by an aggregate score of 32-1. (The one run scored on a wild pitch). Surely, they would be unstoppable against a Yankees team that needed the help of a 12-year-old fan, Jeffrey Maier, to win the ALCS. In Game 1, Maier leaned over the fence of the right-field seats to snatch Derek Jeter's long drive away from Baltimore right fielder Tony Tarasco, a play that was ruled a home run.

To reach Yankee Stadium for the Friday workout, the Braves endured a two-hour delay in rainy Atlanta and a horrific, traffic-infested trip from Newark International Airport. But they had to get there. Just to see what it looked like. Manager Bobby Cox, a third baseman for the Yankees in the late 1960s, stood and marveled at The House That Ruth Built. "That Babe was some architect," joked third baseman Chipper Jones. Greg Maddux said he had such indelible memories of the stadium from old newsreels, "I thought it would be in black and white."

The Braves were loose, sky-high and ready to go. The opening Saturday was lost to a raging thunderstorm that dumped nearly five inches of rain on the New York area, but they hardly broke stride. With Yankee Stadium celebrating its first World Series in 15 years, the Braves turned Game 1 into a 12-1 rout and rode Maddux' shoulders to a 4-0 win in Game 2. These were the Braves in all their glory: A blistering Fred McGriff homer off the right-field foul pole. The relentless pressure applied by Marquis Grissom and Mark Lemke at the top of the order. Thinking-man's pitches on the outer corners of the plate. And one very sudden surprise.

As the St. Louis playoff series drew to a close, Cox was gaining confidence in a 19-year-old outfielder named Andruw Jones. Raised on the tiny island of Curacao, some 40 miles north of Venezuela, Jones had been one of the most publicized Minor League players of the previous two years. He had a stunning, five-tool package that had scouts comparing him to Clemente and Aaron. And now he was walking into Yankee Stadium and hitting two home runs in Game 1: towering, monstrous shots to left field off Pettitte and Brian Boehringer. He was the youngest player ever to go deep in the World Series—a year younger than Mickey Mantle in 1952—and suddenly, the Braves were not merely great. They looked a little scary, as well.

"That was one of the most awesome performances I've ever witnessed," said Lemke. "To do that, at that age, with the pressure of Yankee Stadium? What else compares?"

At this point, the Braves had won five straight Post Season games by a combined score of 48-2. The Atlanta newspapers were claiming victory, comparing the Braves to the great teams of history, and a *New York Post* headline announced, "End of the World." The formidable Tom Glavine was due to pitch Game 3 in Atlanta, and as Torre said, "We've got guys like Smoltz, Maddux and Glavine in our league. It's just that they're not all on the same team."

The Yankees had reached the point of humiliation, and it didn't help to watch Cox give some of his pitchers a casual workout in the middle of a World Series. He let Denny Neagle, his Game 4 starter, pitch an inning of Game 1. Later that night, with an 11-run lead, Cox summoned reliever Brad Clontz to get the last out of the ninth.

"At that point," recalled Cone, "we were just props in the World Series." Mariano Duncan, the Yankees' second baseman and spiritual leader, said, "Nobody in the clubhouse could believe how bad we looked in the first two games."

Torre recalled a conversation he'd had with Steinbrenner after the demoralizing opener. "Joe, tomorrow night is a must game!" Steinbrenner roared. "Must game!"

"Well, it really *isn't* a must game, George," Torre replied. "We look a little rusty. We could lose that game. But don't worry, Atlanta's my town. We'll go down there and win three straight. Then we'll come back up here and win it Saturday night."
Steinbrenner gave his manager sort of a dazed look, then walked away, muttering to himself. "I was really just kidding," said Torre. "Turns out I was dead right."

From the utter chaos of Yankee Stadium, where more than a half-dozen lunatics charged onto the field in the late innings of Game 2, the Series moved on to calm, sedate Atlanta. This would be the final go-round for 30-year-old Fulton County Stadium, soon to be torn down in favor of a new ballpark (the 1996 Olympic track stadium) under renovation nearby. For the first time in history, a ballpark said farewell with a World Series in progress. It was hard to decide which was more stunning: the Braves' three straight losses, or the manner in which they unfolded.

As we look back, the Series' complexion changed in a single moment. Joe Torre came to the mound, David Cone told him a well-meaning fib, and the Braves were never the same.

It was the bottom of the sixth inning, Game 3, bases loaded, the Yankees leading 2-0. Cone had been magnificent, a big-game pitcher true to his reputation. But he had just walked Chipper Jones, and here came McGriff. The percentages looked bad.

Most managers would have gone to the left-handed pitcher, no questions asked. Torre wasn't so sure. He wanted to see Cone up close. Wanted to hear his words, look into his eyes. "Joe got as close as he could to me, face to face," said Cone, "and implored me to be honest with him. And I did my best to lie. I told him I had enough to get through the inning."

Baseball's most successful bullpen was waiting in the wings, along with logic, the percentages and a million second-guessers. But Torre liked what he saw. He enjoyed the passion of Cone's plea. If nothing else, Joe Torre knows loyalty and the human spirit. He stuck with Cone. McGriff popped up. The Yanks were back.

There were many other facets to New York's 5-2 victory. Bernie Williams cracked an RBI single and a two-run homer. Strawberry defied the Braves' exaggerated defensive shift with an opposite field, RBI single. Lloyd, the Aussie from the sheep ranch, retired McGriff and Klesko in an eighth-inning crisis. But it all came back to Cone, who picked up the biggest Yankees victory since the triumphant World Series of '78. "It was a joy to watch Coney tonight," marveled Wetteland. "What he did was . . . so Cone-esque."

What happened the following night, in Game 4, was the greatest single-game comeback in World Series history. The Yankees were trailing 6-0 through five innings, and those knowing glances had returned in the Fulton County Stadium press box. Neagle had a masterpiece going. McGriff had homered. Young Andruw Jones had doubled home a run. Fans were tomahawk-chopping like never before.

Things began to unravel in the sixth, when the Yanks chased Neagle with a three-run rally, but a seminal moment arrived in the eighth. That's when Jimmy Leyritz timed a hanging slider from Mark Wohlers, the most feared relief pitcher in the National League, and tied the game with a three-run homer over the left-field fence. That's when exuberant Yankees poured out of the dugout and a nation realized that the Braves might be vulnerable, after all.

The game lurched on into extra innings; at 4:17, it would be the longest World Series game ever played. By the time Torre sent up Boggs to pinch-hit for infielder Andy Fox with the bases loaded in the 10th, there was nobody left in reserve. Not even a relief pitcher. Torre's next option would have been Cone, or Key, or maybe Don Zimmer in disguise.

It was Boggs against Steve Avery, a badly slumping legend against a sore-armed lefty. And here was the beauty for the Yankees: They didn't need a trademark Boggs single up the middle. They didn't need the long ball. All they needed was his batting eye.

With a 1-and-2 count, Avery threw a dandy slider on the outside corner. Just outside. He threw another one. Barely missed. Now Boggs had the upper hand. A flustered Avery threw a pitch that wasn't close, and the Yanks had their go-ahead run in what became an 8-6 victory.

People marveled at Boggs' concentration on those borderline pitches. They wondered if he feared the worst because a National League umpire, Steve Rippley, was working home plate. "Never crossed my mind," said Boggs. "The ball still has to cross the little white house."

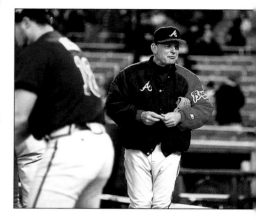

17

And here was the beauty for the Yankees: They didn't need a trademark Boggs single up the middle. They didn't need the long ball. All they needed was his batting eye.

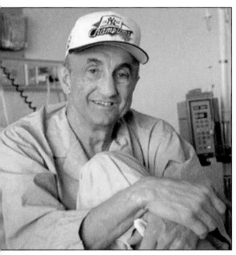

There was an air of nostalgia to Game 5, the last night at Fulton County Stadium. There were memories of Francisco Cabrera, Henry Aaron's 715th, Dale Murphy, Biff Pocoroba and a million Phil Niekro knuckleballs. The fans got another classic, their third in a row, but this was a 1-0 loss so stunning that they just stood in silence after the final out. Nobody stormed the field. Nobody tried to steal second base or rip out a seat. A crowd of 51,881 was left to fathom the pitching of young Andy Pettitte and a single misplay—a break in communication between center fielder Marquis Grissom and right fielder Jermaine Dye—that led to the Yankees' only run in the fourth inning. Paul O'Neill made the last play, somehow managing an all-out sprint on his bum leg to haul down Luis Polonia's drive off Wetteland, and the Yankees were going home with a 3-2 Series lead.

As the Yankees returned home that Friday, it seemed impossible that their remarkable story could get better. But it did. Frank Torre got his heart. You'd have thought that some Hollywood film mogul had barged into the hospital, demanding that the transplant take place before Game 6, or that Steinbrenner had pulled a few strings. But there were no special considerations, no secret dealings with the Yankees in mind. Like Jimmy Leyritz' home run, Wade Boggs' walk and Joe Torre's World Series, it happened naturally—and right on time.

"This is getting unbelievable," said Torre. "I mean, this is like an out-of-body experience for me." He smiled and shook his head. "And wouldn't you know it—the donor was from the Bronx."

The Yankees still had to beat Greg Maddux on a still, perfect evening at the Stadium, and over the course of 7 2/3 innings, they managed just one productive inning. But it was swift and thrilling, a three-run third inning fueled by Girardi's long, run-scoring triple to deep center field. The fabled old yard was rocking, pulsating, as Girardi steamed into third. The young catcher said he was so overwhelmed by the moment, "I almost burst into tears right there." Then came Jeter's single for a 2-0 lead, and another RBI single from Bernie Williams. One big inning. One for the ages. It was all the Yankees needed in a 3-2 victory behind Key, three middle relievers and, ultimately, the closer.

Wetteland wound up getting the save in all four Yankees victories. He became the first reliever to win the Series' MVP award since Rollie Fingers in 1974. But before he could soak up all that glory, he had to retire Mark Lemke—the Braves' gritty second baseman playing in his 24th World Series game—with two runners on. Wetteland ran a full count. Torre could hardly stand to watch. Lemke hit a pop foul to the third-base side, and third baseman Charlie Hayes flew recklessly into the Braves' dugout like a man falling down a flight of stairs. He banged up his knee and his chin—not that he felt the pain—and came within inches of catching the ball.

Torre wanted to visit Wetteland right then, maybe settle him down a little. Then came a voice from Zimmer, Torre's bench coach, the 47-year baseball lifer. "Don't worry," said Zimmer. "The next one's for Frank."

Astonishingly, Lemke hit another foul popup to Hayes. This one stayed on the field. Playable. Hayes pulled it down, leaped joyously into the air, and triggered what might have been the most impressive victory celebration in World Series history.

In truth, it took a massive police force to make it happen. But once it became apparent that only two or three fans were even considering a dash to the field, New York lived up to its reputation: the biggest, the best, the classiest. A place that rises to the occasion. Fans swayed back and forth together, some of them holding hands, singing along with Sinatra's "New York, New York." The players celebrated within a protective circle of mounted police, and once they grasped the perfection of the moment, they didn't want to leave. Zimmer got the idea of a victory lap; Strawberry and Leyritz set it in motion. And suddenly the entire Yankees roster was trotting around the ballpark, not unlike Cal Ripken the night he broke Lou Gehrig's endurance record.

"The fans made it happen," said Leyritz, his voice hoarse from shouting. "They stayed put. They let us all share the moment. They got a chance to thank us, and we thanked them back."

Cone described the scene as "surreal. Guys just seemed to be just floating around the field. The horses were going nuts, the fans were reacting wildly, but it was almost in slow motion."

In a scene that will define that celebration in baseball's video library, Boggs found himself joining one of the cops on horseback. He couldn't quite remember how it happened, because "I'm deathly afraid of horses. Next thing you know, I'm pulling a John Wayne. I was holding on for dear life. I was hoping that horse wouldn't buck me into next week."

The whole thing was unbelievable. The Yanks won the World Series with a .216 team batting average. They were outscored, 26-18. Their team ERA was 3.93 to the Braves' 2.33. Most Valuable Player? It could have been anyone, really. Wetteland, Fielder, Cone, Leyritz, Boggs, Pettitte. Joe Torre. Frank Torre.

"I think I'd vote for the manager," said Strawberry. "His impact is all over this team, and it's all over every player. Joe Torre is the reason we won this World Series."

And so ended a week of excitement, of growing drama, and mostly of healing. The South Bronx had been proud to show off its renewed housing, polished landscape and thriving commerce during the World Series. The city of New York staged a parade that seemed to dwarf all that had come before. In a nation accustomed to hate-the-Yankees sentiment, there could not be universal approval of this World Series. But no one could doubt its compelling nature, what it did for New York's image, or how it served the game of baseball. It will take its rightful place among the best ever played.

19

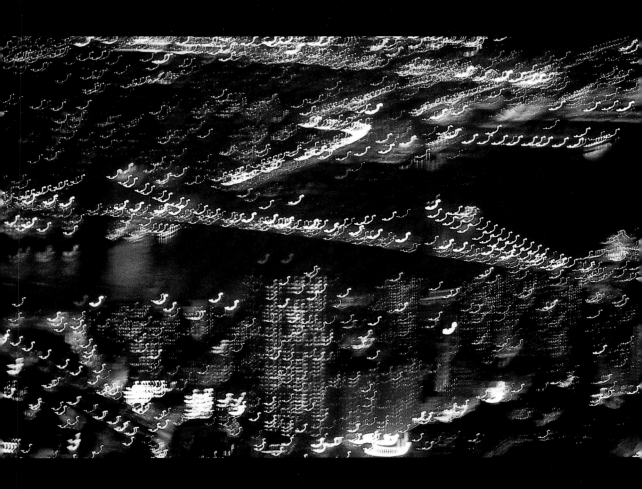

GAME ONE

Game One of the 1996 World Series between the Yankees and the Braves got started a day late due to heavy rains in New York. For the Atlanta Braves, it was another appearance in the Post Season show that had become their own private stage during the 1990s. For the Yankees, it was their first appearance in the title series in 15 years. Before a sell-out crowd in "The House that Ruth Built," the Braves dominated the Yankees, using their trademark great pitching coupled with timely hitting to win Game One by a 12-1 score

"Nothing in our league compares to Yankee Stadium."
—Chipper Jones

After rain postponed Game 1, Yankee Stadium was ready to go on Sunday.

Music, batting practice and equipment checks occupy the time prior to the start of the game. One young fan hopes the Yankees' bubble won't burst as the Series gets underway.

The ceremonial handshake between managers is followed by "The Yankee Clipper," Joe DiMaggio, throwing out the first pitch.

"The tradition and talk at Yankee Stadium is nice, but you can't get caught up in it. You've got to do your job."
—John Smoltz

Andy Pettitte cruised through the first inning, but was rocked by Atlanta in the second. Javier Lopez singled and scored on the first of two Andruw Jones' home runs.

John Smoltz kept the Yankees at bay while his teammates built an 8-0 lead by the fourth. The Yankees outfielders watch as another fresh arm is brought into the game.

"We knew how to pitch Andruw Jones. We knew how to pitch everybody. But every time I had to make a big pitch, I didn't make it."
—Andy Pettitte

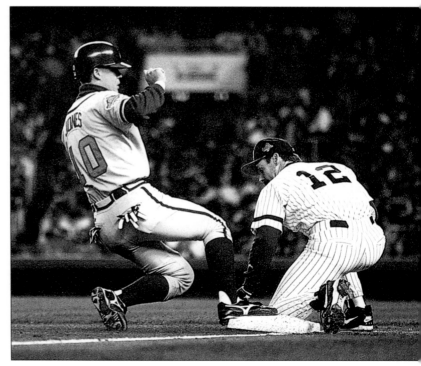

Brian Boehringer relieved Pettitte in the third. He yielded five runs in his three innings of work. Fred McGriff's fifth-inning home run gave the Braves a 9-0 lead.

Light rain couldn't cool the Braves' hot bats. Wade Boggs was back in the Series after a ten-year absence. Denny Neagle threw one scoreless inning. Andruw Jones had an infield single to go with his two home runs.

"I never thought I'd get so far as to hit two home runs in the World Series."
—Andruw Jones, Braves

"We've been on a roll. St. Louis caught us awfully hot those last three games, and the Yankees caught us hot tonight. Hopefully, we can continue it for three more games."
—Bobby Cox

Marquis Grissom tracks down a ball at the wall, and Tino Martinez and Mariano Duncan watch a single roll through the infield. Braves' skipper Bobby Cox and his troops take Game 1 by the score of 12-1.

Atlanta	0 2 6	0 1 3	0 0 0	-12
New York	0 0 0	0 1 0	0 0 0	- 1

Atlanta leads Series 1-0

GAME TWO

At New York
October 21, 1996

Game Two was another cool, efficient thumping of the Yankees by
the Braves. Led by the masterful pitching of Greg Maddux, Atlanta
scratched out single runs in four different innings. The final tally
showed the Braves winning 4-0, while the Yankees, with only one
run scored in Games 1 and 2, were left searching for offensive
answers. Counting the League Championship Series against St.

There's nothing like the sights, sounds and smells of New York City. Artist Andy Jurinko's work (opposite page bottom) showcases the games' best.

"We didn't come in here thinking about winning one game."

—Marquis Grissom

"He (Greg Maddux) is something, he really is. He has his way with you. He was a master tonight."
—Joe Torre

Jimmy Key (opposite) worked six innings, giving up all four Atlanta runs. The Braves scored one run in the first on Mark Lemke's double and Fred McGriff's single. Javier Lopez also singled that inning.

Greg Maddux worked eight innings, surrendering six hits but
no runs. Marquis Grissom doubled and scored the Braves'
second run in the third inning.

"It was a very exciting night."
—Greg Maddux

Mariano Duncan and Derek Jeter (opposite) turn two. Jeter singles. Terry Pendleton rounds second after doubling in the sixth. He later scored the Braves' final run. Jeff Nelson worked 1 $\frac{1}{3}$ innings for New York. Cecil Fielder had two hits in a losing effort.

Jeff Blauser completes a twin-killing (opposite). Tim Raines had a pair of hits from the lead-off spot, but never advanced past first.

"Right now, we need a change of scenery. Things get a little crazy here. There's a lot of pressure." —Paul O'Neill

Jermaine Dye singles. Mariano Rivera shut out Atlanta in the ninth, but it was Mark Wohlers (opposite) who nailed down the win for the Braves.

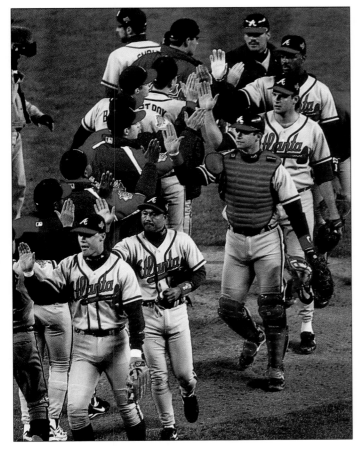

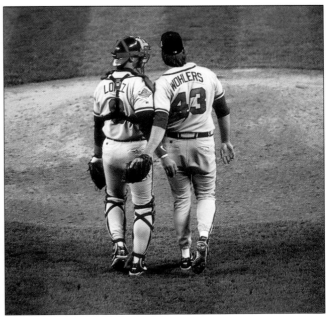

| Atlanta | 1 0 1 | 0 1 1 | 0 0 0 - 4 |
| New York | 0 0 0 | 0 0 0 | 0 0 0 - 0 |

Atlanta leads Series 2-0

GAME THREE

At Atlanta
October 22, 1996

As the Series moved to Atlanta for three games, the Yankees were
facing a "must-win" game. Down 2-0, New York was on the verge
of bowing out of the 1996 Fall Classic with embarrassing haste.
But in Atlanta, with the Tomahawk Chop in full force, the
Yankees got good pitching from David Cone, an RBI single by
Darryl Strawberry and a two-run homer by Bernie Williams to
beat Atlanta 5-2. The stories of the Yankees demise were put on
hold . . . at least for another night.

There was confidence in the air as the Series moved south to Atlanta.

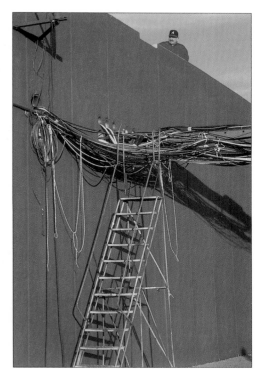

Former President Jimmy Carter and All-Time Home Run King Henry Aaron.

Jim Leyritz hoped to tattoo the ball in Atlanta. Brett Butler, who used to play for the Braves, visited with Darryl Strawberry. The Braves' pair of Joneses, Andruw (below) and Chipper (opposite above).

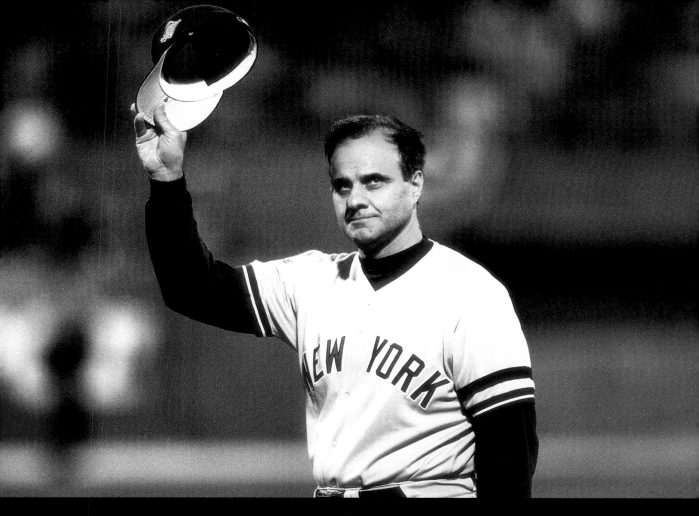

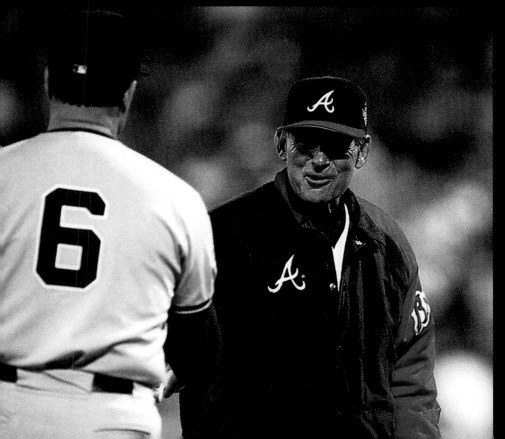

Atlanta-Fulton County Stadium was hosting its last games. Joe Torre doffs his cap to the crowd. He played and managed in Atlanta. Torre and his counterpart, Bobby Cox, meet before Game 3.

"I trust David Cone. I just wanted him to level with me, that was the only thing. I said to him, 'It's very important here. I gotta know if you're OK.' He said, 'I'm fine.'"
—Joe Torre

Tom Glavine pitched seven innings and gave up only one earned run. Andruw Jones went to the wall to make a nice catch. Darryl Strawberry had a single and one RBI. David Cone earned the Yankees first win. Tim Raines was doubled off of first.

Tom Glavine walked and scored in the sixth. Javier Lopez pounces from behind the plate, while Fred McGriff watches a ball roll foul.

"Joe just got as close as he could to me—face to face—and implored me to be honest with him. And I did my best to lie and tell him that I had enough to get through the sixth."
—David Cone

Joe Girardi tracks a pop-up. David Cone completed another inning on the way to the win. Mariano Duncan had his only hit of the Series in Game Three.

"We got down here and heard people talking about the Braves place in history. I'm thinking, 'Already?'"
—David Cone

Bernie Williams (opposite) had scored two runs, and drove in three, including two on his eighth-inning homer. Cecil Fielder had a solid double in the Yankees' three-run eighth.

Brad Clontz gave up a run-scoring single to Luis Sojo in the eighth that made the score 5-1.

A disappointed Braves fan
watched as Graeme Lloyd and
John Wetteland secured the
Yankees' first win.

| New York | 1 0 0 | 1 0 0 | 0 3 0 - 5 |
| Atlanta | 0 0 0 | 0 0 1 | 0 1 0 - 2 |

Atlanta leads Series 2-1

GAME FOUR

At Atlanta
October 23, 1996

Game Four of the World Series will go down in history as a classic. Through five innings, the Braves led 6-0 and seemed to be back in control of this Series. But a funny thing happened on the way to the coronation: The Yankees decided to show everyone why they were champions of the American League. They scored three runs in the sixth and another three in the eighth—on a dramatic home run by Jim Leyritz—then won it in the tenth with two runs. The Series was now knotted at 2-2, and the once-mighty Braves no longer looked invincible.

Yankees starter Kenny Rogers takes his hacks prior to Game 4. Yankees executive Reggie Jackson knows October as well as anyone. Olympic softball gold-medalist Dot Richardson joins in the pre-game festivities.

Prior to the game, Joe Torre and Don
Zimmer share a laugh, as do a relaxed
Greg Maddux and Eddie Perez.

Denny Neagle started for the Braves, lasting five innings. New York starter Kenny Rogers was rocked for five runs in two-plus innings. In the Braves four-run second, Fred McGriff homered and Javier Lopez, who walked, scored on Jeff Blauser's bunt single.

"This team's got heart, that's all I can say. We've been doing this all year; it's not like we invented it in the playoffs."
—Wade Boggs

Yankees starter Kenny Rogers
struggled, thanks in part to Jeff Blauser
and Marquis Grissom. Opposite,
Chipper Jones singled and scored in the
third, as Kenny Rogers searched for
answers.

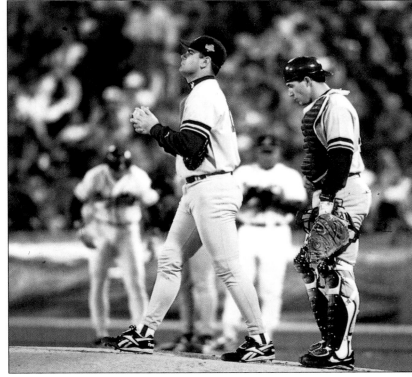

Brian Boehringer threw two solid
innings to slow down the Braves,
who led 5-0 after three innings.
Mark Lemke turns two in the
fourth to shut down New York.

Andruw Jones had three hits and an RBI for the Braves. Derek Jeter singled and scored the Yankees first run in the sixth.

Kirby Puckett (right), one of the game's most beloved players, was honored by Major League Baseball prior to the game.

"The trademark of concentration is thinking of nothing."
—Wade Boggs

Cecil Fielder's single in the sixth drove in Derek Jeter. With three runs in, Braves' Manager Bobby Cox decided to end the evening for starter Denny Neagle.

Jeff Nelson hurled two great innings to give the Yankees a chance to come back. Darryl Strawberry and Charlie Hayes had singles to set the stage in the dramatic eighth inning.

Mike Bielecki gave the Braves two
shutout innings. Derek Jeter contributed
a pair of hits in the game.

Jim Leyritz (opposite) was the unlikely hero in Game 4, hitting a three-run, eighth-inning homer to knot the game at 6-6. With the bases loaded, Steve Avery walked Wade Boggs on a 3-2 pitch to give the Yankees a 7-6 lead in the tenth.

"We know we're going back to New York. And we don't know if that's good news or bad."
—Joe Torre

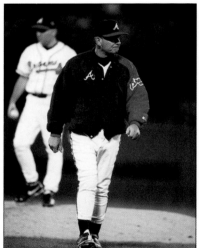

Bobby Cox brought in Brad Clontz in the tenth after Boggs drew his RBI walk. Clontz induced Charlie Hayes to pop-up to first, but Ryan Klesko was blinded by the lights and the ball fell to the ground, allowing Derek Jeter to score the inning's second run.

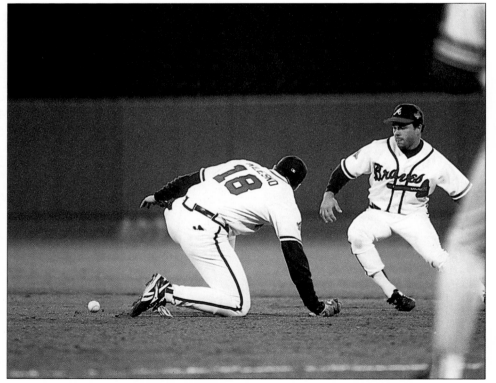

John Wetteland secures the win and his second save in a row. Joe Torre and his Yankees have now battled back from a 2-0 hole to tie the Series at two games each.

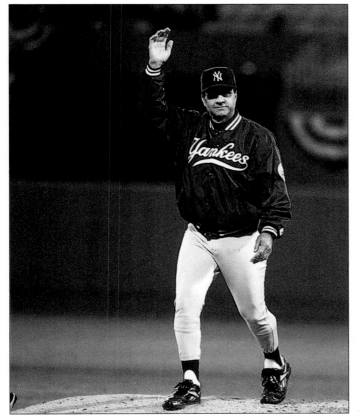

New York	0 0 0	0 0 3	0 3 0	2 - 8						
Atlanta	0 4 1	0 1 0	0 0 0	0 - 6						

The Series is tied 2-2

GAME FIVE

At Atlanta
October 24, 1996

It's possible that in the history of baseball, there has been
a more exciting pitchers' duel than the one that took place
during Game Five in Atlanta. But it's not likely. With the
Series knotted at 2-2, Atlanta's John Smoltz faced New
York's Andy Pettitte, and the two showed why they were
their league's top winners in 1996. Smoltz worked eight
innings, allowing one unearned run, while Pettitte
worked 8 1/3 innings of no-run ball for the victory. The
sole run scored through little fault of Smoltz, the result of
an error by Marquis Grissom

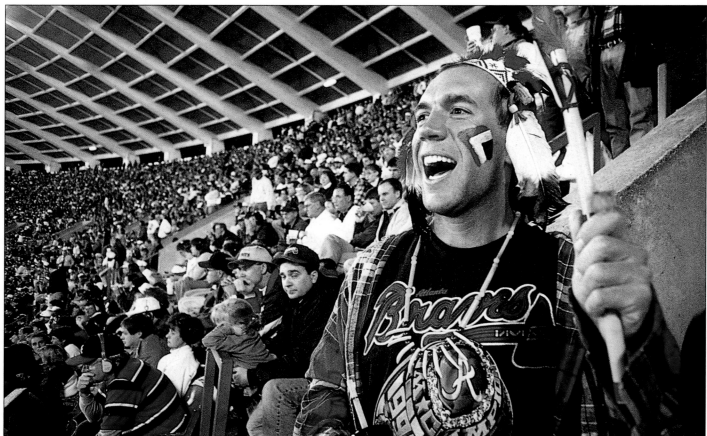

John Smoltz pitched
a spectacular game,
going eight innings
and allowing four
hits and one run.
Unfortunately he
faced Andy Pettitte
(opposite), who shut
down the Braves for
eight-plus innings.

*"That was the best I've ever pitched,
considering the circumstances."*
—John Smoltz

In the fourth, Charlie Hayes' drive to right was played poorly by Marquis Grissom and Jermaine Dye, allowing Hayes to coast into second. Bernie Williams advanced Hayes to third (right), and Cecil Fielder drove him home with a double.

"Error on me. E-8, OK? Y'all seen it."
    —Marquis Grissom

"The crowd noise was so loud, I didn't hear him until the last second."
    —Jermaine Dye

Cecil Fielder, not known for his blazing speed, amuses Mark Lemke after chugging into second base. Charlie Hayes scored the game's only run.

Jim Leyritz and Andruw Jones had a
hit each in this pitchers' duel.

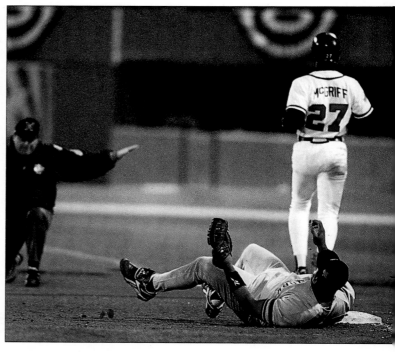

Marquis Grissom knocked out a pair of hits. Jim Leyritz walked and stole second in the seventh, but he was out when Andy Pettitte's poor bunt hung him out between second and third. In Atlanta's seventh, Fred McGriff was safe on Derek Jeter's error. But he was erased when Javier Lopez hit into a fielder's choice (opposite). Mark Wohlers cleans up for the Braves. Andy Pettitte paces as John Wetteland goes for his third save in a row.

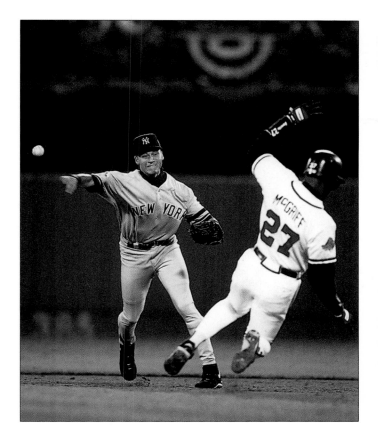

Mariano Duncan's stolen base (opposite) and Paul O'Neill's walk amounted to nothing in the ninth. John Wetteland earned the save, but not before Luis Polonia flied out to Paul O'Neill in deep right with a runner on third.

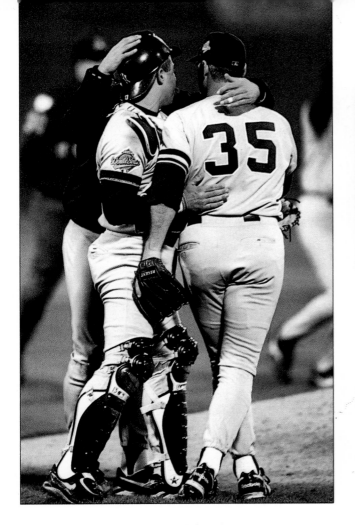

*"We just saw three straight
classics. I wouldn't mind being a
writer right now. Pick a story line
and go with it."*
—David Cone

114

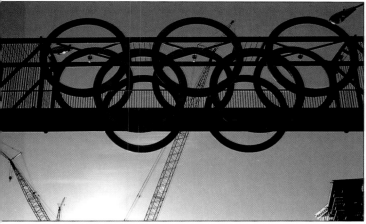

With Game 5, Atlanta-Fulton County Stadium closed down forever, ending a 31-year run. In 1997, the Braves will call the modified Olympic Stadium their home.

New York	0	0	0	1	0	0	0	0	0	-1
Atlanta	0	0	0	0	0	0	0	0	0	-0

New York leads Series 3-2

GAME SIX

At New York
October 26, 1996

Back in New York for Game Six, the Braves could only hope that the trend of this Series would continue: neither team yet had won a game at home. Destiny was with the boys from Gotham. The Yankees put together only one scoring inning, scoring three runs in the third, but Yankees starter Jimmy Key and four relievers made it stand up. When Atlanta's Mark Lemke popped out to Charlie Hayes at third to complete the Yankee's 3-2 win, New York was on top of the baseball world.

118

Back in the Bronx, the Yankees hoped to have all the tools to polish off their foes from the South.

"There's so many human stories in this clubhouse. You can truly say it's a New York team."
—George Steinbrenner

Bobby Cox and Bernie Williams have on their game faces. Wayne Gretzky (opposite) shows his true colors. Prior to the game, fans get a chance to wish their favorite players luck.

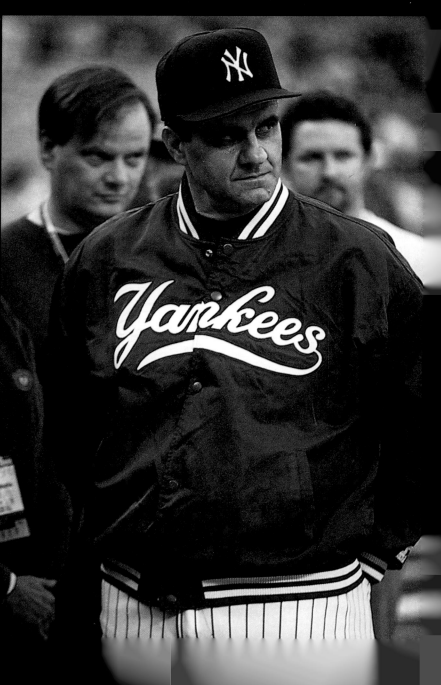

Wade Boggs and Joe Torre hope
to close out the Series in Game
Six. Spike Lee, ever the
filmmaker, shoots some home
video before the game.

"So much emphasis has been put on our pitching rotation that people assume it's going to be easy. On paper, it looks great. But people don't know what goes on in the trenches, what it takes to win baseball games."
—John Smoltz

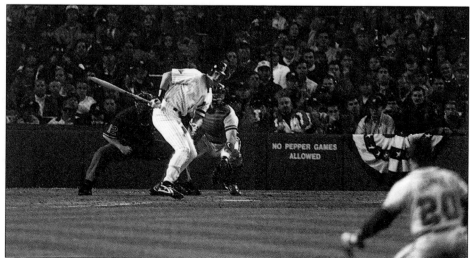

Jimmy Key (opposite top) started for the Yankees. He held the Braves to one run before leaving in the sixth. Paul O'Neill (opposite bottom) doubled to right to start the Yankees three-run rally in the third inning. Joe Girardi tripled in O'Neill, then Derek Jeter singled to drive in Girardi.

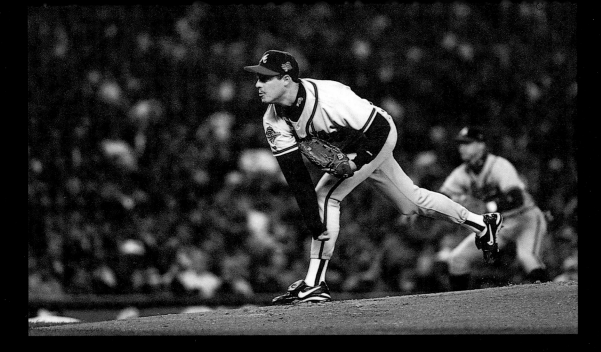

Greg Maddux only had one bad inning, but it was enough to give the Yankees all the runs they needed. Bernie Williams drove in the final run in the third with a single.

127

Greg Maddux gets some advice from batterymate Javier Lopez. Lopez had a single to help in the Braves fourth, when they scored a single run.

"This is the most overachieving team I've ever been a part of."
—Tino Martinez

Terry Pendleton grounded into a DP to end Atlanta's chances in the fourth. Marquis Grissom's one-out single in the fifth looked like the start of a promising inning.

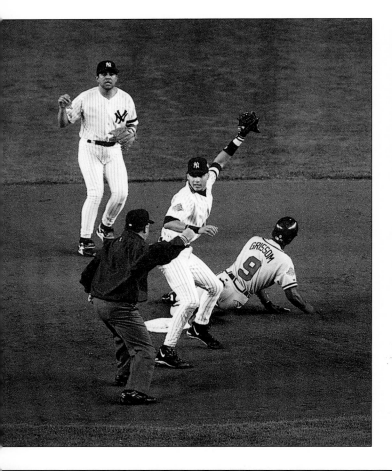

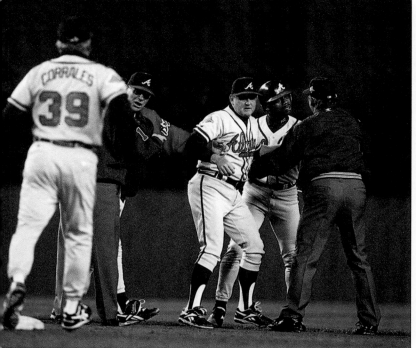

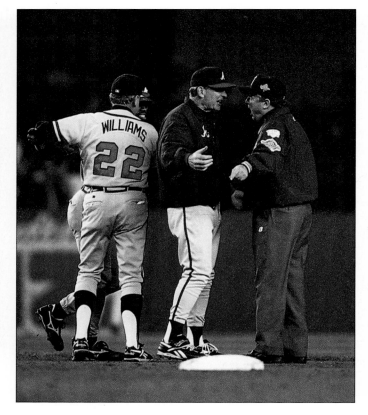

Marquis Grissom was out at second on a fielder's choice.
Manager Bobby Cox was unhappy with Tim Welke's call, and
let him know about it. Apparently, the Braves' skipper was a
bit too pointed in his critique of the call, and Welke ejected him.

After Chipper Jones doubled to right and was moved to third by Fred McGriff in the sixth, Jimmy Key was through for the evening.

David Weathers relieved Jimmy Key. He was followed to the mound by Graeme Lloyd, who induced Ryan Klesko to pop out to Luis Sojo to end the inning.

"Now I know how Neil Armstrong felt when he walked on the moon."
—Wade Boggs

"We had our chance. We just didn't get it done. It's as simple as that."
—Fred McGriff

Mariano Rivera worked two scoreless innings in a set-up role. Jeff Blauser turns two in the seventh to erase a leadoff walk.

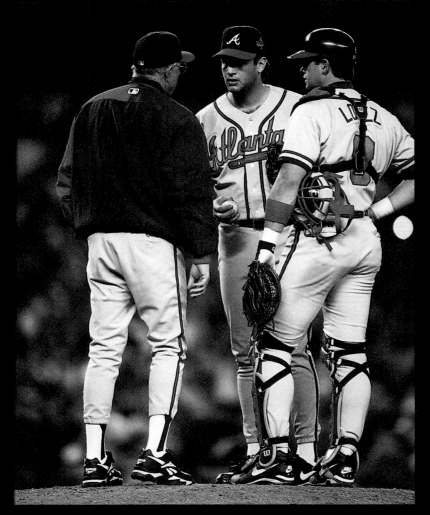

Mark Wohlers (left) got the last out for Atlanta. John Wetteland (bottom left) recorded his fourth straight save, but not before surrendering three hits and one run. Charlie Hayes squeezes the final out.

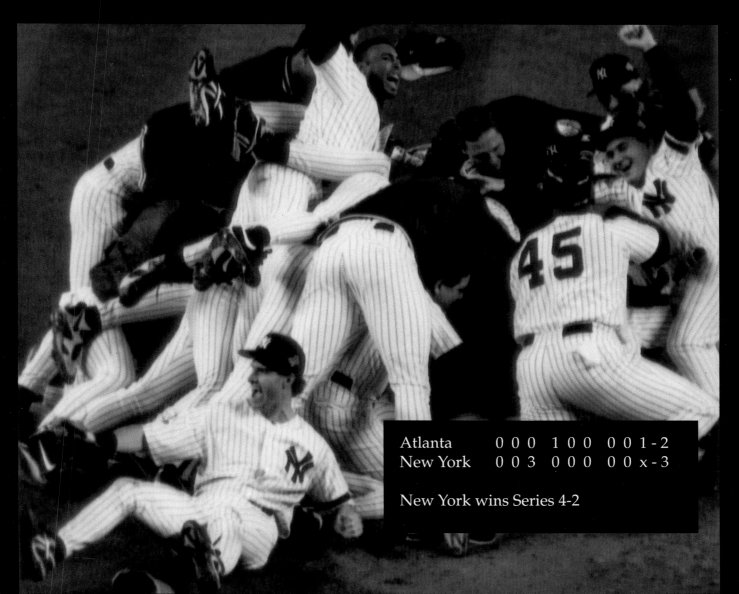

| Atlanta | 0 0 0 | 1 0 0 | 0 0 1 - 2 |
| New York | 0 0 3 | 0 0 0 | 0 0 x - 3 |

New York wins Series 4-2

WORLD CHAMPS!

Yanks beat Braves to take Series

Faces of champions (opposite page, clockwise): Jimmy Key and his fiancée; Joe Torre and Yankees GM Bob Watson; Joe Torre and George Steinbrenner with New York Mayor Rudolph Giuliani. (This page, clockwise): Series' Most Valuable Player John Wetteland; Joe Torre; Mariano Duncan; Andy Pettitte.

Mayor Giuliani gives the key to the city to Bernie Williams and the rest of the hometown heroes. More than three million delighted New Yorker's cheered their champions.

THE WORLD SERIES IN NUMBERS

GAME ONE

Atlanta	ab	r	h	bi
Grissom cf	5	2	2	1
Lemke 2b	4	0	2	1
CJones 3b	4	1	1	3
McGriff 1b	5	2	2	2
Lopez c	4	2	1	0
Perez c	0	0	0	0
Dye rf	5	0	1	0
AJones lf	4	3	3	5
Klesko dh	4	1	0	0
Blauser ss	3	1	1	0
Polonia ph	1	0	0	0
Belliard ss	0	0	0	0
Totals	39	12	13	12

New York	ab	r	h	bi
DJeter ss	3	1	0	0
Boggs 3b	4	0	2	1
BeWilliams cf	3	0	0	0
Martinez 1b	3	0	1	0
Fielder dh	4	0	0	0
Strawberry lf	3	0	0	0
Raines lf	1	0	0	0
O'Neill rf	2	0	0	0
Aldrete rf	0	0	0	0
Hayes ph	1	0	0	0
Duncan 2b	3	0	0	0
Fox 2b	0	0	0	0
Sojo ph	1	0	0	0
Leyritz c	3	0	1	0
Totals	31	1	4	1

Atlanta	0 2 6	0 1 3	0 0 0	—12
New York	0 0 0	0 1 0	0 0 0	—1

E-Duncan (1). LOB-Atlanta 3, New York 8. 2B-Boggs (1). HR-McGriff (1), AJones 2 (2). RBIs-Grissom (1), Lemke (1), CpJones 3 (3), McGriff 2 (2), AJones 5 (5), Boggs (1). SB-CJones (1). S-Lemke. SF-CJones.

Atlanta	IP	H	R	ER	BB	SO
Smoltz W (1-0)	6	2	1	1	5	4
McMichael	1	2	0	0	0	1
Neagle	1	0	0	0	0	0
Wade	.2	0	0	0	0	0
Clontz	.1	0	0	0	0	0

New York	IP	H	R	ER	BB	SO
Pettitte L (0-1)	2.1	6	7	7	1	1
Boehringer	3	5	5	3	0	2
Weathers	1.2	1	0	0	0	0
JNelson	1	1	0	0	0	1
Wetteland	1	0	0	0	0	2

T-3:02. A-56,365 (57,545). Umpires-HP, Evans; 1B, Tata; 2B, Welke; 3B, Rippley; LF, Young; RF, Davis.

GAME TWO

Atlanta	ab	r	h	bi
Grissom cf	5	1	2	1
Lemke 2b	4	2	2	0
CJones 3b	3	0	1	0
McGriff 1b	3	0	2	3
Lopez c	4	0	1	0
Dye rf	4	0	1	0
AJones lf	3	0	0	0
Pendleton dh	4	1	1	0
Blauser ss	2	0	0	0
Polonia ph	1	0	0	0
Belliard ss	0	0	0	0
Totals	33	4	10	4

New York	ab	r	h	bi
Raines lf	4	0	2	0
Boggs 3b	4	0	1	0
BeWilliams cf	4	0	0	0
Martinez 1b	4	0	0	0
Fielder dh	4	0	2	0
Fox pr	0	0	0	0
O'Neill rf	4	0	1	0
Duncan 2b	3	0	0	0
Girardi c	3	0	0	0
DJeter ss	2	0	1	0
Totals	32	0	7	0

Atlanta	1 0 1	0 1 1	0 0 0	—4
New York	0 0 0	0 0 0	0 0 0	—0

E-Raines (1). LOB-Atlanta 7, New York 6. 2B-Grissom (1), Lemke (1), CJones (1), Pendleton (1), O'Neill (1). RBIs-Grissom (2), McGriff 3 (5). CS-Raines (1). S-Lemke. SF-McGriff. DP Atlanta 1; New York 2.

Atlanta	IP	H	R	ER	BB	SO
Maddux W (1-0)	8	6	0	0	0	2
Wohlers	1	1	0	0	0	3

New York	IP	H	R	ER	BB	SO
Key L (0-1)	6	10	4	4	2	0
Lloyd	.2	0	0	0	0	2
JNelson	1.1	0	0	0	0	2
MRivera	1	0	0	0	0	1

HBP-by Maddux (DJeter), by Key (AJones). T-2:44.
A-56,340 (57,545). Umpires-HP, Tata; 1B, Welke; 2B, Rippley; 3B, Young; LF, Davis; RF, Evans.

GAME THREE

New York	ab	r	h	bi
Raines lf	4	1	1	0
DJeter ss	3	1	1	0
BeWilliams cf	5	2	2	3
Fielder 1b	3	0	1	0
Fox pr	0	1	0	0
Martinez 1b	0	0	0	0
Hayes 3b	5	0	0	0
Strawberry rf	3	0	1	1
Duncan 2b	3	0	1	1
Sojo 2b	1	0	1	1
Girardi c	2	0	0	0
Cone p	2	0	0	0
Leyritz ph	1	0	0	0
MRivera p	1	0	0	0
Lloyd p	0	0	0	0
Wetteland p	0	0	0	0
Totals	33	5	8	5

Atlanta	ab	r	h	bi
Grissom cf	4	1	3	0
Lemke 2b	4	0	1	1
CJones 3b	3	0	1	0
McGriff 1b	3	0	0	0
Klesko lf	3	0	0	1
Lopez c	4	0	1	0
AJones rf	4	0	0	0
Blauser ss	4	0	0	0
Glavine p	1	1	0	0
Polonia ph	0	0	0	0
McMichael p	0	0	0	0
Clontz p	0	0	0	0
Bielecki p	0	0	0	0
Pendleton ph	1	0	0	0
Totals	31	2	6	2

New York	1 0 0	1 0 0	0 3 0	—5
Atlanta	0 0 0	0 0 1	0 1 0	—2

E-DJeter (1), Blauser (1). LOB-New York 9, Atlanta 7. 2B-Fielder (1), 3B-Grissom (1). HR-BeWilliams 3 (3). RBIs-BeWilliams 3 (3), Strawberry (1), Sojo (1), Lemke (2), Klesko (1). CS-AJones (1), Polonia (1). S-DJeter, Girardi. DP-New York 1, Atlanta 1.

New York	IP	H	R	ER	BB	SO
Cone W (1-0)	6	4	1	1	4	3
MRivera	1.1	2	1	1	1	1
Lloyd	.2	0	0	0	0	1
Wetteland S (1)	1	0	0	0	0	2

Atlanta	IP	H	R	ER	BB	SO
Glavine L (0-1)	7	4	2	1	3	8
McMichael	0	3	3	0	0	0
Clontz	1	1	0	0	1	1
Bielecki	1	0	0	0	2	2

IBB-off Clontz (Strawberry (1). McMichael pitched to 3 batters in the 8th
T-3:22. A-51,843 (52,710). Umpires-HP, Welke; 1B, Rippley; 2B, Young; 3B, Davis; LF, Evans; RF, Tata.

ATLANTA BRAVES

PLAYER	G	AB	R	H	2B	3B	HR	RBI	BB	SO	AVG.
Smoltz	1	2	0	1	0	0	0	0	0	0	.500
Grissom	6	27	4	12	2	1	0	5	1	2	.444
AJones	6	20	4	8	1	0	2	6	3	6	.400
McGriff	6	20	4	6	0	0	2	6	5	4	.300
CJones	6	21	3	6	3	0	0	3	4	2	.286
Lemke	6	26	2	6	1	0	0	2	0	3	.231
Pendleton	4	9	1	2	1	0	0	0	1	1	.222
Lopez	6	21	3	4	0	0	1	1	3	4	.190
Blauser	6	18	2	3	1	0	0	1	1	4	.167
Dye	5	17	0	2	0	0	0	0	1	1	.118
Klesko	5	10	2	1	0	0	0	1	2	4	.100
Mordecai	1	1	0	0	0	0	0	0	0	0	.000
Bielecki	2	1	0	0	0	0	0	0	0	1	.000
Glavine	1	1	1	0	0	0	0	0	1	1	.000
Neagle	1	1	0	0	0	0	0	0	0	1	.000
Perez	2	1	0	0	0	0	0	0	0	0	.000
Polonia	6	5	0	0	0	0	0	0	1	2	.000
Wohlers	3	0	0	0	0	0	0	0	0	0	—
Belliard	4	0	0	0	0	0	0	0	0	0	—
McMichael	1	0	0	0	0	0	0	0	0	0	—
Clontz	2	0	0	0	0	0	0	0	0	0	—
Avery	1	0	0	0	0	0	0	0	0	0	—
Maddux	0	0	0	0	0	0	0	0	0	0	—
Wade	1	0	0	0	0	0	0	0	0	0	—
TOTALS	6	201	26	51	9	1	4	26	23	36	.254

PITCHER	G	IP	H	R	BB	SO	HB	W	L	ERA
Bielecki	2	3	0	0	3	6	0	0	0	0.00
Clontz	3	1.2	1	0	1	2	0	0	0	0.00
Wade	2	.2	0	0	1	0	0	0	0	0.00
Smoltz	2	14	6	2	8	14	0	1	1	0.64
Glavine	1	7	4	2	3	8	0	0	1	1.29
GMaddux	2	15.2	14	3	1	5	1	1	0	1.72
Neagle	2	6	5	3	4	3	0	0	0	3.00
Wohlers	4	4.1	7	3	2	4	0	0	1	6.23
Avery	1	.2	1	2	3	0	0	0	0	13.50
McMichael	2	1	5	3	0	1	0	0	0	27.00
TOTALS	6	54	43	18	26	43	1	2	4	2.33

Complete games—none. Saves—none.